There was a scarecrow in the field next to the wood. It wore a dark blue jacket, a pair of blue trousers and a pair of brown boots. It was sad because it did not scare the crows.

Wellington liked the scarecrow. He tried to help it by running around the field barking at the crows. He did not scare them either. They jumped up in the air and laughed at him.

Then one day Wellington went to the field and the scarecrow was not there. The crows were flying round and round, high in the air, looking for it.

Wellington ran all over the field. Where was the scarecrow? He could not find it. Then he saw one of its boots in a corner. There was a trail of straw coming from it.

There was a trail of straw all the way into the wood. Did Wellington dare to follow it? Yes. Wellington was brave. He went into the wood.

Wellington carefully followed the trail of straw. He saw a hare running between a pair of trees. He saw a rare green woodpecker on the trunk of an oak tree.

Then he saw a pair of trousers by a bush. They were the scarecrow's trousers. He saw a jacket. It was the scarecrow's jacket. Wellington carefully went up to the bush to peep round it.

He saw a fox with a pair of cubs snuggled in the straw in the scarecrow's jacket. Wellington stared at them. They did not know he was watching them.

Wellington did not disturb them. He turned round to go back home. Just then he saw the scarecrow's hair sticking up in the long grass. Then he saw its face. Wellington looked at it.

The scarecrow had a smile on its face. It did not look sad anymore. It was taking care of the baby foxes. It was happy. Wellington felt happy for it too.

"are"

dare   scarecrow

hare   rare

scare   care

stared carefully

"air"

air   hair   pair

there   where